Invasion of Species by Ballast Water

A Comprehensive Guide into Ballast Water Treatment Systems, its Effects and Current Situation

Sunil Sarangi

TABLE OF CONTENTS

CHAPTER 1
HISTORY OF BALLAST WATER

Ballast water is essential for the safe operation of ships. It provides stability and maneuverability during a voyage and during loading and unloading operations. Ships are designed and built to move through water carrying cargo, such as oil, grains, containers, machinery and people. If the ship is traveling without cargo, or has discharged some cargo in one port and is on route to its next port of call, ballast water may be loaded on board to achieve the required safe operating conditions. Among others this includes keeping the ship deep enough in the water to ensure efficient propeller and rudder operation.

Ballast is weights added to a ship to improve stability, balance, and trim. In the past, this was often rocks found nearby a port. For flexibility, ships today pump water in and out of tanks as ballast – Ballast Water. Ballast water is taken onboard when cargo is unloaded and discharged when cargo is loaded or can be added for extra stability in foul weather.

By example, the container vessel Emma Mærsk, built in 2013, carries over 11,000 standard containers each weighing up to 20 tons and has 60,000 cubic meters (15.8 million gallons) of tank capacity set aside for ballast water. As the cargo is offloaded, that weight is replaced with a like quantity of ballast water. When the ship arrives at another port for loading, the ballast water is pumped from the tanks. In this way, water is transported from one locale and released in another. However, ballast water contains more than just plain water. When ballast water is taken into a ship, so are local species.

When the ship travels to it's loading port, these species are discharged along with the ballast water. The environmental conditions are similar for port to port, but the natural predators are not. Since ports are often located at the mouths of rivers and in bays where plentiful nutrients support hardy species, populations of a new species can grow to invasive levels. Good examples are the zebra mussels in the Great Lakes, Quagga mussels on the West Coast, mitten crabs in the San Francisco Bay, and the blue crab in Northern Europe. Whether it is along a seaboard or across an ocean, the release of ballast water brings unintended consequences.

Legislation

The worldwide extent of the unintended transport of invasive species has become a focal point for environmental legislation. National governments are inclined to limit the movement of non-indigenous species throughout the world. In 2004, the delegates to the International Maritime Organization (IMO) drafted a set of regulations for the control of the movement of invasive species known as the International Convention for the Control and Management of Ship's Ballast Water and Sediment, or Ballast Water Management Code (BWM Code).

The BWM Code provides two primary regulations intended to reduce the transport of invasive species: "Regulation D-1, Ballast Water Exchange" and "Regulation D-2, Ballast Water Treatment." Regulation D-1 seeks to reduce invasive species by flushing the majority of them out before arriving at a different port. Regulation D-2 requires the installation of new shipboard systems to remove invasive species to specified levels. The systems of Regulation D-2 are to be verifiable, record operational time, note instances when bypassed, and allow for sampling of the treated ballast water (effluent).

At its inception, the BWM Code was to go into effect when it had been ratified by at least 30 countries with 35% of the world's tonnage. On September 9, 2016, Finland ratified the BWM Code, bringing the Convention into force with 52 nations and 35.14% of the world's tonnage in agreement.

Along with the BWM Code, the United States government – in this case, the United States Coast Guard (USCG) – has given consideration to the impact of invasive species. The USCG issued a final rule on their position in November 2015 – applying Regulation D-2 standards but on a different time table.

The International Convention for the Control and Management of Ships' Ballast Water and Sediments (Ballast Water Management Convention or BWM Convention) is a 2004 international maritime treaty which requires signatory flag states to ensure that ships flagged by them comply with standards and procedures for the management and control of ships' ballast water and sediments. The Convention aims to prevent the spread of harmful aquatic organisms from one region to another and halt damage to the marine environment from ballast water discharge, by minimising the uptake and subsequent discharge of sediments and organisms. From 2024 all ships are required to have approved Ballast Water Management Treatment System, according to the D2 standard. Existing ships are required to install an approved system, which may cost up to 5 million USD per ship to install. To assist with implementation the IMO has released 14 Guidance documents in regards to the Convention including the G2 Guidelines for Ballast Water Sampling, G4 Guidelines for Ballast Water management and G6 Guidelines for Ballast Water Exchange.

The first scientifically recognised occurrence of a non-indigenous marine species being transported in ships water occurred in the North Sea in 1903, with the Asian phytoplankton Odontella appearing. The issue became more prevalent with the increase in shipping in the late 20th century and the issue was raised for the first time at the IMO in 1988.Following several years of development, the Convention was adopted by the International Maritime Organization in 2004. To enter into force, the Convention required ratification by a minimum of 30 States, representing 35% of world merchant shipping tonnage, subject to which it would enter into force 12 months later.On 8 September 2016, Finland acceded to the Convention, bringing the contracting states to 52 and the combined tonnage of States to 35.14%. This triggered the applicability of the entry into force date of the Convention, which occurred on 8 September 2017. Since Finland, a number of States have continued to ratify the treaty, bringing the total as of November 2018 to 78 contracting States, representing 77.19 per cent of world merchant shipping tonnage.

Under the Convention, ships are required, according to a timetable of implementation, to comply with the D1 or D2 standards. The D1 standard requires ships to carry out a ballast water exchange, and specifies the volume of water that must be replaced. This standard involves exchanging the uptaken discharge water from the last port, with new sea water; it must occur at a minimum of 200 nautical miles from shore. The D2 standard is more stringent and requires the use of an approved ballast water treatment system. The system must ensure that only small levels of viable organisms remain left in water after treatment so as to minimise the environmental impact of shipping.

New ships will be required to install and comply with the D2 standard from the 8th September 2017, once the Convention has entered into force. Existing ships, who are subject to the phased implementation schedule, have potentially (depending on the renewal of their ship certificates) until the 8th September 2024, by which time all ships will comply with the D2 standard.

It is also possible for ships to discharge ballast at approved shore reception facilities in ports, as article 5 requires that when cleaning or repair of a ships ballast tanks occurs, ports should have adequate reception facilities for the sediments.Facilities must include safe disposal arrangements, storage and treatment equipment, safe and suitable mooring and emergency arrangements and the necessary reducers for connections to ships.

Some ships may be exempted from complying with the Convention, according to certain conditions and the appropriate permission being given by a flag State. These include ships trading in a limited area, small vessels including sailboats and fishing vessels, vessels only operating on one coast and also FPSOs.

The Technology to Outfit Ships

With deadlines for compliance approaching, there will be increased demand for these new technologies to be installed. For instance, a ship with a ballast water capacity of 1400 cubic meters built 1969 would be required by the USCG and IMO to be retrofitted with a ballast water treatment system not later than 2021 (2016 implementation + 5 years maximum time between dry-docking).

Technologies for treatment systems which are currently showing promise include filtration with some type of sanitization – Ozone, ultraviolet irradiation, biocides, and hydrogen peroxide to name a few – along with a monitoring and control system.

The technology to treat ballast water is required to go through an approval process in order to be suitable for installation. It is a three-stage process – theoretical analysis, controlled testing and onboard testing. For the USCG acceptance of ballast water treatment, the controlled testing must be done at a facility approved by the USCG.

As of September this year, 50 systems were in process through both the IMO and USCG testing cycles, with six (6) systems having been fully approved by the USCG.

Ballast water treatment systems will not offer a 'one size fits all' approach, as the system for a given ship will need to address that ship's particular needs for through-put, total ballast capacity, duration of ballast retention, trade route and a myriad of other variables.

Now that the BWM Code has achieved international mandate, the pressure is on for system designers, operators, reviewers, and installers.

CHAPTER 2
POLLUTION CAUSED BY BALLAST WATER

Ballast water discharges by ships can have a negative impact on the marine environment. The discharge of ballast water and sediments by ships is governed globally under the Ballast Water Management Convention, since its entry into force in September 2017. It is also controlled through national regulations, which may be separate from the Convention, such as in the United States.

Cruise ships, large tankers, and bulk cargo carriers use a huge amount of ballast water, which is often taken on in the coastal waters in one region after ships discharge wastewater or unload cargo, and discharged at the next port of call, wherever more cargo is loaded. Ballast water discharge typically contains a variety of biological materials, including plants, animals, viruses, and bacteria. These materials often include non-native, nuisance, exotic species that can cause extensive ecological and economic damage to aquatic ecosystems, along with serious human health issues including death.

There are hundreds of organisms carried in ballast water that cause problematic ecological effects outside of their natural range. The International Maritime Organization (IMO) lists the ten most unwanted species as:

- Cholera Vibrio cholerae (various strains)

- Cladoceran Water Flea Cercopagis pengoi

- Mitten Crab Eriocheir sinensis

- Toxic algae (red/brown/green tides) (various species)

- Round Goby Neogobius melanostomus

- North American Comb Jelly Mnemiopsis leidyi

- North Pacific Seastar Asterias amurensis

- Zebra Mussel Dreissena polymorpha

- Asian Kelp Undaria pinnatifida

- European Green Crab Carcinus maenas

- Other problematic species include:

- Spiny Water Flea Bythotrephes longimanus

To react to the growing concerns about environmental impact of ballast water discharge, the International Maritime Organization (IMO) adopted in 2004 the "International Convention for the Control and Management of Ships' Ballast Water and Sediments" to control the environmental damage from ballast water. The Convention will require all ships to implement a "Ballast water management plan" including a ballast water record book and carrying out ballast water management procedures to a given standard. Guidelines are given for additional measures then the guidelines.

The goals of the convention are to minimise damage to the environment by:

- Minimise the uptake of organisms during ballasting.

- Minimising the uptake of sediments during ballasting.

- Ballast water exchange while at sea (the ship should be minimum 200 nautical miles from shore with a depth of minimum 200 metres and can use the flow through or sequential method). At least 95 percent of the total ballast water should be exchanged.

- Treatment of the ballast water by chemical or mechanical influences (UV-radiation, filter, deoxygenation, cavitation, ozone…)

Control measures include:

- International Ballast Water Management Certificate

- Ballast water management plan

- Ballast water record book

The IMO convention was ratified by enough countries and entered into force on September 8, 2017.

Ballast water is essential for safe and efficient modern shipping operations. But ballast water also impacts serious ecological problems due to the multitude of marine species carried in ships' ballast water. The ballast water includes bacteria, microbes, small invertebrates, eggs, cysts and larvae of various species.

The transferred species may survive to establish a reproductive population in the host environment, becoming invasive species. At the end the ballast water impacts native species that may be multiplying into pest proportions.

Water has a good weight-to-volume ratio and is carried in separate tanks used just for ballast, or in empty cargo tanks. When a vessel is departing a port, water and any sediment that may be stirred up, is loaded into the ballast tanks and unloaded again when it takes on cargo at the next port. However, the process of loading and unloading untreated ballast water poses a major threat to the environment and public health as ballast water impacts the transfer of organisms between ecosystems, from one part of the world to another.

How does the Ballast Water Impact?

When ballast water is loaded many microscopic organisms and sediments are introduced into the ships ballast tanks. Many of these organisms are able to survive in these tanks. Ballast water impacts the environment when the ballast water is discharged and the organisms are released into new environments. If suitable conditions exist in this release environment, these species will survive and reproduce and become invasive species. In some cases there is a high probability that the organism will become a dominant species, potentially resulting in:

- The extinction of native species

- Effects on local and regional biodiversity

- Effects on coastal industries that use water extraction

- Effects on public health

- Impacts on local economies based on fisheries

Ballast Water Impacts the Biodiversity

The problem of invasive species in ships' ballast water is largely due to the expanded trade and traffic volume over the last few decades and, since the volumes of seaborne trade continue to increase, the problem may not yet have reached its peak yet. The effects in many areas of the world have been devastating. Actually invasive aquatic species are one of the four greatest threats to the world's oceans. Quantitative data show that the rate of bio-invasions is continuing to increase at an alarming rate and new areas are being invaded all the time.

But how exactly does the ballast water impact the biodiversity? Species from the ballast water are considered alien if they are not native to a given ecosystem. They are also referred to as non-native species. Alien species are considered to be invasive when their introduction causes, or is likely to cause, harm to the environment, the economy, or human health.

The introduction and spread of alien invasive species is a serious global threat to marine and freshwater ecosystems. New species may completely alter the local communities, drive species to extinction as well as cause economic damage as nuisance species.

Results of the Ballast Water Impacts

New non-native species are constantly being discovered in Scandinavia. This is partly explained by the increase in trade and travel. Climate change is indeed another important factor. With generally higher temperatures, a longer growing season, and shorter, milder winters, it will become easier for alien species to establish populations in Scandinavia. These are species that could have serious impacts on ecosystems and threaten native Scandinavian species if they become established.

Examples of actual and possible effects of non-native aquatic animals which have recently been introduced to Scandinavia from shipping are shown below:

- Round Goby. The round goby poses a serious threat to the Scandinavian aquatic ecosystems, with potential impacts on commercial fishing. Since its discovery in the Baltic Sea, this bottom-dwelling fish has rapidly spread to many areas.

- Comb Jellyfish. The invasion of the Baltic Sea by a voracious comb jellyfish from North America is one of the best-documented examples of a marine alien invasive species introduced through ballast water. It eats both zooplankton, the food of commercially important fish, and the eggs and larvae of the same fish species.

- Chinese Mitten Crab. The Chinese mitten crab has been found all over the coastal Baltic Sea and also in some adjacent rivers and lakes. It outcompetes native species of crayfish for food and space, and can cause a decline in the populations of native species.

How can the Ballast Water Impacts Cause Damage?

Many alien species are unable to adapt to a new environment or are harmless if they do survive, but others pose a threat to native plants and animals. They may for instance:

- Compete with native species for food and/or habitat

- Alter the habitat in which they live

- Carry diseases or parasites

- Hybridism with native species

- Increase the risk that already threatened species will become extinct, or displace native species from an area

It should be noted that ballast water has been disposed by ships in ports, harbours and coastal waters since the early 1900's and that during this time many non-native species have been introduced. However, recognizing the possible severity of the ballast water impacts, organizations are now taken action by developing guidelines for preventing the introduction of non-native species which aim to minimise the effects.

Invasive Aquatic Species in ship's ballast water is one of the biggest problems faced by the shipping industry. Posing a great threat to the marine ecosystem, these aquatic species has led to an increase in bio-invasion at an alarming rate. Under IMO's "International Convention for the Control and Management of Ship's Ballast Water and Sediments", implementation of ballast water management plan and ballast water treatment system on board ships has thus become important.

In order to ensure their ships comply with the rules and regulations set by IMO regarding Ballast Water Management, several shipping operators have started implementing ballast water treatment systems on their ships.

A variety of technologies are available in the market for treating ballast water on ships. However, constraints such as availability of space, cost of implementation, and level of environmental friendliness play an important role in usage of a particular type of ballast water treatment system.

A number of factors are taken into account for choosing a ballast water treatment system for a ship. Some of the main factors taken into consideration are –

- Effectiveness on ballast water organisms

- Environment-friendliness

- Safety of the crew

- Cost effectiveness

- Ease of installation and operation

- Space availability on board

The main types of ballast water treatment technologies available in the market are:

- Filtration Systems (physical)

- Chemical Disinfection (oxidizing and non-oxidizing biocides)

- Ultra-violet treatment

- Deoxygenation treatment

- Heat (thermal treatment)

- Acoustic (cavitation treatment)

- Electric pulse/pulse plasma systems

- Magnetic Field Treatment

A typical ballast water treatment system on board ships use two or more technologies together to ensure that the treated ballast water is of IMO standards.

Physical Separation/ Filtration Systems Ballast Water Treatments

Physical separation or filtrations systems are used to separate marine organisms and suspended solid materials from the ballast water using sedimentation or surface filtration systems. The suspended/filtered solids and waste (backwashing) water from the filtration process is either discharged in the area from where the ballast is taken or further treated on board ships before discharging.

Ballast Water Filtration

The following equipment are mainly used for ballast water filtration:

Screens/Discs: Screens (fixed or movable) or discs are used to effectively remove suspended solid particles from the ballast water with automatic backwashing. These are extremely environmentally friendly as they do not require usage of toxic chemicals in the ballast water. Screen filtration is effective for removing suspended solid particles of larger size but is not very handy in removing particles and organisms of smaller sizes.

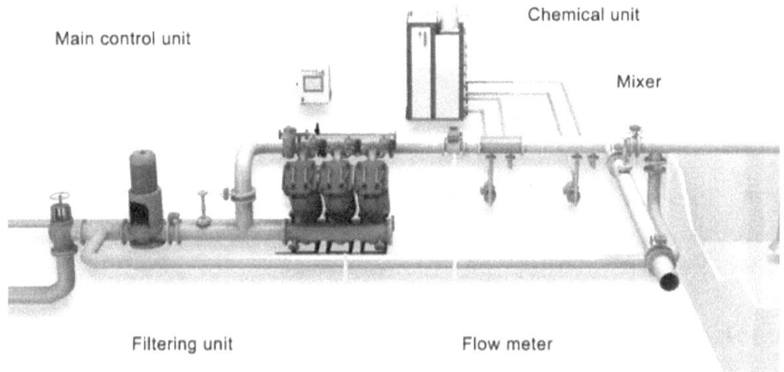

How Ballast Water Treatment System Works?

Invasive Aquatic Species in ship's ballast water is one of the biggest problems faced by the shipping industry. Posing a great threat to the marine ecosystem, these aquatic species has led to an increase in bio-invasion at an alarming rate. Under IMO's "International Convention for the Control and Management of Ship's Ballast Water and Sediments", implementation of ballast water management plan and ballast water treatment system on board ships has thus become important.

In order to ensure their ships comply with the rules and regulations set by IMO regarding Ballast Water Management, several shipping operators have started implementing ballast water treatment systems on their ships.

A variety of technologies are available in the market for treating ballast water on ships. However, constraints such as availability of space, cost of implementation, and level of environmental friendliness play an important role in usage of a particular type of ballast water treatment system.

A number of factors are taken into account for choosing a ballast water treatment system for a ship. Some of the main factors taken into consideration are –

- Effectiveness on ballast water organisms

- Environment-friendliness

- Safety of the crew

- Cost effectiveness

- Ease of installation and operation

- Space availability on board

Ship Deballasting

The main types of ballast water treatment technologies available in the market are:

- Filtration Systems (physical)

- Chemical Disinfection (oxidizing and non-oxidizing biocides)

- Ultra-violet treatment

- Deoxygenation treatment

- Heat (thermal treatment)

- Acoustic (cavitation treatment)

- Electric pulse/pulse plasma systems

- Magnetic Field Treatment

A typical ballast water treatment system on board ships use two or more technologies together to ensure that the treated ballast water is of IMO standards.

Physical Separation/Filtration Systems Ballast Water Treatments

Physical separation or filtrations systems are used to separate marine organisms and suspended solid materials from the ballast water using sedimentation or surface filtration systems. The suspended/filtered solids and waste (backwashing) water from the filtration process is either discharged in the area from where the ballast is taken or further treated on board ships before discharging.

The following equipment are mainly used for ballast water filtration:

Screens/Discs: Screens (fixed or movable) or discs are used to effectively remove suspended solid particles from the ballast water with automatic backwashing. These are extremely environmentally friendly as they do not require usage of toxic chemicals in the ballast water. Screen filtration is effective for removing suspended solid particles of larger size but is not very handy in removing particles and organisms of smaller sizes.

Note: It has been noticed that though screens are highly effective in removing majority of suspended solid particles and organisms from ballast water, they alone are not sufficient to treat the ballast water according to IMO standards.

Hydrocyclone: Hydrocyclone is an effective equipment for separating suspended solids from the ballast water. High velocity centrifugal force is used to rotate the water to separate solids. As hydrocyclone doesn't have a moving part, it is easy to install, operate and maintain on board ships.

Note: It has been found that as the operation of hydrocyclone heavily depends on the mass and density of the particle, they are not successful in removing smaller organisms from the ballast water.

Coagulation: As most of the physical filtration methods are not able to remove smaller solid particles, the method of coagulation is used prior to the filtration process to join smaller particles together to increase their size. As the size of the particles increase, the efficiency during the above mentioned filtration processes increases. Such treatment involving coagulation of smaller particles into small flocs is known as flocculation. The flocs settle more quickly and can be removed easily.

Note: Some ballast water treatment systems using coagulation and flocculation utilize ancillary powder (sand, magnetite etc.) or coarse filters to produce flocs. An additional tank is required for treating ballast water for this process and thus extra space is required on board ships.

Media Filters: Physical ballast water treatment systems with media filters can also be used in order to filter out smaller sized particles. It has been found that compressible media filters (Crumb rubber) are more suited for shipboard use because of their compact size and lower density as compared to conventional granular filtration systems.

CHAPTER 3
DANGERS OF BALLAST WATER AND REVENUE LOSS TO FISHERIES

Shipping plays a crucial role in supporting global trade, including the transport of products from the aquaculture industry. However, ships may also unintentionally transport invasive species and pathogens in their ballast water which pose biosecurity risks for aquaculture. The Ballast Water Management Convention was developed to manage the biosecurity risks posed by ballast water and has entered into force in September 2017. The management measures and technologies arising from the convention provide some solutions and opportunities for the aquaculture industry. Among these is the potential transfer of treatment technologies between shipping and aquaculture in order to deal with bio-invasion and biosecurity. However, there are residual weaknesses in the regulatory regimes for ballast water management which may reveal a continuous risk from shipping to the aquaculture industry. Gaps include knowledge and management of other aquatic bacteria or viruses that could cause outbreaks in the aquaculture industry and threaten food security and human health. Solutions include focused risk assessments for aquaculture and regional collaboration.

Naturally, this global trade also includes the trade of fish meals, animal feeds and aquaculture Products. Nearly 40 % of fish output (wild caught and farmed) is traded internationally, making seafood one of the most extensively traded commodities in the world. It is considered that exports of fish products from developing countries represent a larger proportion of total exports compared to that of tropical beverages, nuts, spices, cotton and sugar combined. In this respect, the aquaculture industry is dependent on the capacity of shipping to transport these goods and products, and at reasonable prices. There is however, another linkage between these two industries, and that is the biosecurity risks posed by the global movement of ships which may unintentionally transport pathogens with the potential to affect aquaculture. There is a need to understand and evaluate how these two industries are inherently connected. In this paper, we offer an overview of the existing regulatory regimes developed by the member states participating in the global objectives of the International Maritime Organization (IMO) as well as the United States of America's Coast Guard to decrease the risks of transfer of pathogens. We focus on the management tools and frameworks dealing with the risks associated with the transport of ballast water and eventually reflect on the potential transfer of technologies between shipping and aquaculture in order to deal with bio-invasion and biosecurity.

Because of the consequences of bio-invasions generated by the exchange of ballast water across ecosystems, this topic has received quite a bit of attention in the last decades, and much research on organisms transferred through ballast water or its sediments has been carried out.

Ballast water is estimated to be responsible for the transfer of between 7 000 and 10 000 different species of marine microbes, plants and animals globally, each day.

The annual amount of ballast water transported is large; estimated to be between 3.5 billion tonnes and 10 billion tonnes. Large ships such as bulk carriers may pump 10 000 to 20 000 of water per hour. Relating this to a traditional pond size in the Asian shrimp industry, this would equate to 1–3 shrimp ponds per hour.

The International Maritime Organization (IMO), with its headquarters in London, has come up with a list of the ten most unwanted marine species carried by ballast water

Ballast Water Management

To address the issue of biological invasions through shipping, the IMO has worked towards the development of a regulatory regime which provides measures to protect the environment from bio-invasions. This includes the Guidelines for the control and management of ships' biofouling to minimize the transfer of invasive aquatic species which are intended to provide a globally consistent approach to the management of biofouling.

In 1991, the Marine Environment Protection Committee (MEPC) of the IMO adopted the International guidelines for preventing the introduction of unwanted aquatic organisms and pathogens from ships' ballast water and sediment discharges through the resolution MEPC.50 (31). A few years later in 1997, the developments and discussion generated from these first guidelines supported the IMO-MEPC in adopting the Guidelines for the control and management of ships' ballast water to minimize the transfer of harmful aquatic organisms and pathogen through the resolution A 868(20). Eventually, the International Convention for the Control and Management of Ships' Ballast Water and Sediments was adopted in 2004 through the resolution MEPC.253 (67).

This last resolution is also referred to as the Ballast Water Management Convention, or BWMC. As a convention and not a guideline, this last is legally binding. The convention was to enter into force exactly one year after at least 30 countries representing 35 % of the world merchant shipping tonnage have ratified it. In order to prepare for the convention to enter into force, there has been a large amount of work carried out by IMO. To support the preparation of stakeholders to the entry into force of the convention, the GEF-UNDP-IMO GloBallast Partnerships Programme was developed. This programme was initiated in late 2007 and was intended to be finished in 2012, but has been extended until the spring of 2017.

Asian Fisheries Science 31S (2018)

Following the ratification of the convention by Finland in September 2016, the BWMC has entered into force in September 2017. The world merchant fleet is now bonded to the convention. This entry into force will ensure that a good part of the bio-invasion risks associated with ballast water exchanges will be managed and reduced.

Further issues of ballast water and marine pollution

The world's oceans are under threat, under threat from marine pollution, from over-fishing and from physical destruction. As if this is not enough, they are also under threat from alien invaders, marine species transported beyond their natural range and dispersed across the globe by shipping.

Shipping moves over 80% of the world's commodities and transfers around 10 billion tonnes of ballast water each year. Ballast is absolutely essential to the safe and efficient operation of ships, providing balance and stability when empty of cargo. However, it may also pose a serious ecological, economic and health threat.

The problem arises when ballast water contains marine life. There are literally thousands of species that may be carried in ships' ballast - anything small enough to pass through a ship's ballast water intake pumps. This includes bacteria, small invertebrates and the eggs, cysts and larvae of various species.

The development of larger, faster ships combined with rapidly increasing world trade means that the natural barriers to the dispersal of species across the oceans are being reduced. As a result, whole ecosystems are being changed and economic impacts can be massive. In one example from North America, the introduced European Zebra Mussel has infested over 40% of internal waterways and has required over US$5 billion in expenditure on control measures since 1989. In several countries, introduced, microscopic, 'red-tide' algae have been absorbed by filter-feeding shellfish, such as oysters. When eaten by humans, these contaminated shellfish can cause paralysis and even death. The list goes on, hundreds of examples of major ecological, economic and human health impacts across the globe. It is even feared that cholera may be transported in ballast water.

In many cases ships with ballast water on board are changing exotic species between various continents as a kind of travelling fish tank. The impact from ballast water is not only noticeable on environmental and economic terms, the spread of some exotic species could have a negative effect on public health in some cases. For example, a little worm in ballast water could lead to a spread to the disease cholera.

If we compare the spread of exotic species with oil pollution, then we see that oil pollution is visible, has a major media impact, is it initiating political reactions and usually restores the environment after some time. If we are looking to the spread of exotic species, then we see that these will arise undetected and will often increase very largely.

Although the spread of exotic species will arise undetected, the consequences are almost irreversible. The Chinese mitten crab is a good example of this. This kind of non-native species originally came from Asia, which you now find at the Dutch coast.

The Chinese mitten crab, which you now can find in the brackish and fresh water of the Benelux, poses a major threat to many indigenous species. For example, the Chinese mitten crabs are not that much picky when it comes to food. Besides that, their pincers take care of serious economic damage for fishing and fyke nets, but also for the stability of the dams.

The greatest hazards created by a ship's ballast water are the invasive species carried from one region to another. These species, which include viruses and bacteria naked to the human eye, forms of algae, mussels, clams and crabs, are impossible to eradicate once they establish a foothold. This threat is so large it is viewed as one of the top threats to the world's oceans.

In the Caspian and Black Seas, a very small form of jellyfish was transported from its natural habitat thousands of miles away in the Atlantic

Ocean where its population was balanced with its natural predator, to an area where it flourished with nothing to stop it. This has completely ruined the once thriving fishing industry, leaving ports deserted and the people that depend on the industry in poverty.

In other areas of the world, invading mussels have attached themselves to pumps in dams and power plants, posing a real threat to the inhabitants of the communities that depend on these structures. Red algae transported in ballast water is proven to be extremely toxic and immediately eradicates all living marine life except the clams, that if fed to humans are poisonous and cause death. For more information on the global hazards of ballast water, and the new Regulations under the Ballast Water Treatment Convention as enforced by the IMO (International Maritime Organization) please see Globallast.imo.org, an organization dedicated to reducing the harmful effects of the transfer of ships' ballast water.

CHAPTER 4
RECOMMENDED SOLUTIONS TO THE NEGATIVE IMPACTS OF BALLAST WATER

A Ballast Water Treatment System (BWTS) can contribute to prevent the negative consequences of ballast water.

The Ballast Water Treatment Convention will enter into full force on September 8, 2017, and all ships will need to have approved ballast water treatment methods on board. Ballast water is seawater used as ballast to balance a ship, and is pumped in or out to add or reduce weight for stability. The problem is that this seawater is picked up in one port, and discharged in another. This introduction of invasive species new to a region are establishing a large presence and wreaking havoc on the ecosystem in a multitude of ways, causing insurmountable damages.

All ships whether cruise, cargo or tankers must comply by September 8, 2017, according to stipulations of the original Ballast Water Treatment Convention which stated that regulations would enter into full force 12 months after receiving ratification from at least 30 member States, or 35% of the world's merchant shipping in tons. Finland's accession on September 8, 2016 has propelled the global enforcement of the Convention, requiring all vessels to utilize effective ballast water treatment methods.

Meanwhile, there are various types of Ballast Water Treatments Systems on the market. For example, ballast water treatment with UV light, a system which injects chloride dioxide into the ballast water as it is loaded and systems based on chemical methods. Also a couple of after-treatment systems are developed. These kind of systems are working, for example, with peracetic acid.

Magnetic Field Treatment

The magnetic field treatment uses the coagulation technology. Magnetic powder is mixed with the coagulants and added to the ballast water. This leads to the formation of magnetic flocs which includes marine organisms. Magnetic Discs are used to separate these magnetic flocks from the water. (Refer the figure above)

Chemical Disinfection (Oxidizing and non-oxidizing biocides) Ballast Water Treatments

Biocides (Oxidizing and non-oxidizing) are disinfectants which have been tested to potentially remove invasive organisms from ballast water. Biocides removes or inactivates marine organisms in the ballast water. However, it is to note that the biocides used for ballast water disinfectant purpose must be effective on marine organisms and also readily degradable or removable to prevent discharge water from becoming toxic in nature.

On the basis of their functions, biocides are mainly divided into two types:

- Oxidizing

- Non-Oxidizing

Oxidizing biocides: Oxidizing biocides are general disinfectants such as chlorine, bromine, and iodine used to inactivate organisms in the ballast water. This type of disinfectants act by destroying organic structures of the microorganisms such as cell membrane or nucleic acids.

Non-oxidizing biocides: Non-oxidizing biocides are a type of disinfectants which when used interfere with reproductive, neural or metabolic functions of the organisms.

More information on biocides can be found below.

Oxidizing Biocides

Some of the processes utilizing oxidizing biocides used on board ships are:

Chlorination – Chlorine is diluted in water to destroy the micro-organisms.

Ozonation – Ozone gas is bubbled into the ballast water using an ozone generator . The ozone gas decomposes and reacts with other chemicals to kill organisms in the water.

Other oxidizing biocides such as chlorine dioxide, peracetic acid, and hydrogen peroxide are also used to kill organisms in the ballast water.

Non-Oxidizing Biocides

Though there are several non-oxidizing biocides available in the market, only a few such as Menadione/ Vitamin K are used in ballast water treatment system as they tend to produce toxic by-products. A lot of research is being made in this field to make more non-oxidizing biodes feasible for use in ballast treatment plant.

Ultra-Violet Treatment Method

Ultraviolet ballast water treatment method consists of UV lamps which surround a chamber through which the ballast water is allowed to pass. The UV lamps (Amalgam lamps) produce ultraviolet rays which acts on the DNA of the organisms and make them harmless and prevent their reproduction. This method has been successfully used globally for water filtration purpose and is effective against a broad range of organisms.

Deoxygenation

As the name suggests, the deoxygenation ballast treatment method involves purging/removing of oxygen from the ballast water tanks to make the organisms asphyxiated. This is usually done by injecting nitrogen or any other inert gas in the space above the water level in the ballast tanks.

Note: It generally takes approximately 2-4 days for the inert gas to asphyxiate the organisms. Thus, this method is usually not suitable for ships having short transit time. Moreover, such type of systems can be used on ships with perfectly sealed ballast tanks. If a ship is already installed with an inert gas system, then a deoxygenation system will not require more space on board ships.

Heat Treatment

This treatment involves heating the ballast water to reach a temperature that will kill the organisms. A separate heating system can be utilized to heat the ballast water in the tanks or the ballast water can be used to cool the ship's engine, thus disinfecting the organisms from the heat acquired from the engine. However, such treatment can take a lot of time before the organisms become inactive and would also increase the corrosion in the tanks.

Cavitation or Ultrasonic Treatment

Ultrasonic energy is used to produce high energy ultrasound to kill the cells of the organisms in ballast water. Such high pressure ballast water cavitation techniques are generally used in combination with other systems.

Electric Pulse / Plasma Treatment

The electric pulse /plasma for ballast water treatment is still in the development stage. In this system, short bursts of energy are used to kill the organisms in ballast water.

In the pulse electric field technology, two metal electrodes are used to produce energy pulse in the ballast water at very high power density and pressure. This energy kills the organisms in the water.

In electric plasma technology, high energy pulse is supplied to a mechanism placed in the ballast water, generating a plasma arc and thus killing the organisms.

Both these methods are said to have almost the same effect on the organisms.

A Typical Ballast Treatment Treatment System on Ships

Most of the ballast water treatment system use 2-3 disinfectant methods together, divided into different stages. A general ballast water treatment plant comprises of two stages with one stage using physical separation while the second stage employing some disinfectant technology. The choice of treatment system used in combination depends on a variety of factors such as type of ship, space available on the ship, and cost limitations as mentioned before.

There have been various forms of ballast water treatment methods from simply exchanging the ballast water while out at sea to on board treatment methods that eradicate any living invasive species, thus carrying and discharging non-threatening water, no matter the region where discharge is necessary. Exchanging the ballast water at sea is not always an option for a ship's captain when in high seas and dropping ballast water would jeopardize the safety of the ship and crew. With the new regulations, ships must be equipped with a complete and effective solution.

There are three approaches to treating ballast water; mechanical, physical or chemical. Mechanical methods would include separation and filtration; physical methods include ozone, electrical currents, or UV radiation, while chemical solutions are biocides or a form of chlorination.

CHAPTER 5
UV RADIATION AS A HEADWAY FOR BALLAST WATER

UV irradiation is performed either by low pressure (LP) or medium pressure (MP) UV lamps. LP lamps emit UV-C radiation, primarily at 254 nm, which is most efficiently absorbed by nucleic acids and causes DNA damages (Sinha and Häder, 2002). UV induced DNA damages can be reversed by DNA repair mechanisms, referred to as photoreactivation and dark repair. MP UV lamps emit radiation spanning the UV-A, -B and -C bands causing additional damage to proteins and enzymes. For instance, UV-B radiation can affect key components in photosynthesis causing energy deprivation in phytoplankton cells. Thus, it has been argued that MP UV lamps can cause a higher degree of inactivation compared to LP UV lamps.

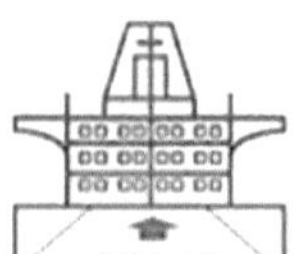

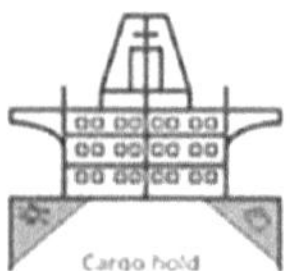

UV irradiation can leave cells in different conditions (live, dead or damaged), whereof the viability of damaged cells at discharge is uncertain.

Damaged cells can be unculturable, though they can be metabolic active and may pose a health risk. Further, cellular DNA repair mechanisms can restore the genetic information causing the cell to grow and replicate after discharge. Additionally, the terminology describing the organisms at discharge can be confusing or unclear. The IMO Convention refers to "viable" organisms, and the Guidelines for approval of ballast water management systems (G8) define "viable organisms" as "organisms and any life stages thereof that are living" (International Maritime Organization, 2008a). USCG also uses the term "living".

Determining the condition of UV irradiated cells is a complex task. On the other hand, cheap, fast and reliable methods to analyze ballast water are necessary for approval of BWTS technologies and for compliance testing of ballast water discharge (International Maritime Organization, 2013). Testing for compliance can be performed in two steps; an indicative and a detailed analyses. An indicative analysis is a relatively simple and quick measurement that gives a rough estimate of the number of viable organisms in the ballast water at discharge. Examples of indicative analysis methods are: e.g. BallastCAM and various fluorescence or ATP detections.

If an indicative analysis shows compliance to Regulation D-2, there is no need for a detailed analysis. Should the indicative analyses be non-compliant, however, a detailed analysis must be undertaken to give robust and direct measurements determining the concentration of viable organism in ballast water discharge according to Regulation D-2. Quantification of live bacteria traditionally relies on cultivation methods, which is time-consuming and may give false negatives as several species are uncultivable although viable. Flow cytometry (FCM) has been suggested as a promising method for detailed analysis (International Maritime Organization. FCM facilitates rapid detection, enumeration and characterization of organisms in combination with fluorescent dyes, and enables to study populations and communities indirectly.

Previously a FCM protocol was developed to distinguish between live and dead Tetraselmis suecica cells. For UV irradiated samples the FCM protocol could not distinguish between live and damaged cells, as the latter contain both dying and repairable cells. The current study uses the FCM protocol to elaborate on different UV doses and the effect of dark incubation on inactivation of the algae T. suecica, to simulate a ballast water treatment and subsequent transport. Our specific objectives were to:

1) Determine the minimum UV dose that permanently inactivates the algae.

2) Quantify effects of different UV doses on T. suecica.

3) Estimate the time of dark incubation required to permanently inactivate the algae treated with UV doses lower than minimum permanently inactivation dose.

4) Provide recommendations for ballast water management.

U.S. Coast Guard and Security Requirement

To ensure the safety of recreational boaters, the U.S. Coast Guard has certain safety requirements for recreational boats up to 65 feet. While most of the safety laws are essentially the same for each size category of boats, some differ.

If your boat is 16–26 feet, you have additional responsibilities compared with the owner of a smaller boat. Knowing the U.S. Coast Guard Safety Regulations will ensure you are in compliance and will help secure your safety and that of your passengers.

State Registration

All recreational boats must be registered in the state where they are most used. When you register your boat, the state will issue you a "certificate of number." You must have the certificate on board while the boat is in use, and the number must be displayed on the outside of the boat. You also have the option to register your boat with the Coast Guard.

State Numbering and Letters

It's not enough to have your certificate of number on board. You must attach the number on each side of the forward half of the boat so that it is visible. The number must be in contrasting color to the boat and at least 3 inches in height. Your state's validation sticker or stickers must be attached within 6 inches of the registration number. Nothing else may be displayed nearby.

Certificate of Documentation

For documented vessels only, an original and current certificate must be on board. The vessel name must be on the exterior part of the hull and must be at least 4 inches in height. The official number, at least 3 inches in height, should be permanently affixed on the interior structure.

Personal Flotation Device

One type of Coast Guard-approved life jacket or life vest must be on board for each person on the boat. You must also have one Type V personal flotation device, like a ring or cushion, that you can throw to someone in the water.

Visual Distress Signal

The Coast Guard requires that boats 16–26 feet have at least one of the following combination of distress signal devices:

- One orange distress flag and one electric distress light

- Three hand-held or floating orange smoke signals and one electric distress light

- Three combinations (day/night) red flares that can be hand-held, meteor, or parachute type

Fire extinguisher

If your boat has an inboard engine, enclosed compartments where fuel or flammable and combustible materials are stored, closed living spaces, or permanently installed fuel tanks, you are required to have one marine-type USCG B-1 fire extinguisher.

Ventilation

If your boat was built after April 25, 1940, and uses gasoline in an enclosed engine or fuel tank compartment, it must have natural ventilation. If it was built after July 31, 1980, it must have an exhaust blower.

Sound-Producing Device

You need a sufficient way to make a sound signal, like a whistle or an air horn, but not a human-produced noise. The sound signals are used when meeting, crossing, or overtaking other vessels, or if visibility is reduced.

Navigation Lights

You must have your navigation lights on between sunset and sunrise and during times of reduced visibility. The U.S. Coast Guard Safety Regulations booklet describes acceptable navigation lightning for different types of recreational boats.

Backfire Flame Arrestor

Gasoline engine boats manufactured after April 25, 1940, are required to have a means of backfire flame control. The exception is those with outboard motors.

Marine Sanitation Device

If your boat has an installed toilet, it must have a Coast Guard-certified operable marine sanitation device. The device can be a Type I or II flow-through or Type III holding tank.

New Coast Guard Rules and Regulations

The International Convention for the Control and Management of Ships' Ballast Water and Sediments (BWM Convention) will enter into force on 8

September 2017, announced by the International Maritime Organisation (IMO). However, the date on which existing ships of 400 GT or more must meet the D2 standard requirements (these covers specifies levels of viable organisms left in water after treatment) have been postponed to 8 September 2019. This is the new date for these vessels that need to renew their IOPP (International Oil Pollution Prevention) certificate to comply with the D2 standard.

An IOPP certificate must be renewed every five years. This means that all existing ships of 400 GT or more must comply with the D2 standard between 8 September 2019 and 8 September 2024. Newbuilding vessels delivered after 8 September 2017 must comply directly with the D2 standard. Vessels below 400 GT must meet the D2 standard on 8 July 2024.

It is expected that many ship owners and shipping companies will choose to install a Ballast Water Treatment System (BWTS) from the moment they must comply with the D2 standard. Berger Maritiem will be pleased to help you with finding, selecting, engineering and installing the right Ballast Water Treatment System for your type of vessel.

The United States Coast Guard (USCG) is the coastal defense, search and rescue, and maritime law enforcement branch of the United States Armed Forces and one of the country's seven uniformed services. The Coast Guard is a maritime, military, multi-mission service unique among the U.S. military branches for having a maritime law enforcement mission (with jurisdiction in both domestic and international waters) and a federal regulatory agency mission as part of its mission set. It operates under the U.S. Department of Homeland Security during peacetime, and can be transferred to the U.S. Department of the Navy by the U.S. President at any time, or by the U.S. Congress during times of war. This has happened twice: in 1917, during World War I, and in 1941, during World War II.

Created by Congress on 4 August 1790 at the request of Alexander Hamilton as the Revenue-Marine, it is the oldest continuous seagoing service of the United States. As Secretary of the Treasury, Hamilton headed the Revenue-Marine, whose original purpose was collecting customs duties in the nation's seaports. By the 1860s, the service was known as the U.S. Revenue Cutter Service and the term Revenue-Marine gradually fell into disuse.

The modern Coast Guard was formed by a merger of the Revenue Cutter Service and the U.S. Life-Saving Service on 28 January 1915, under the U.S. Department of the Treasury. As one of the country's five armed services, the Coast Guard has been involved in every U.S. war from 1790 to the Iraq War and the War in Afghanistan.

The Coast Guard has 40,992 men and women on active duty, 7,000 reservists, 31,000 auxiliarists, and 8,577 full-time civilian employees, for a total workforce of 87,569. The Coast Guard maintains an extensive fleet of 243 coastal and ocean-going patrol ships, tenders, tugs and icebreakers called "cutters", and 1650 smaller boats, as well as an aviation division consisting of 201 helicopters and fixed-wing aircraft. While the U.S. Coast Guard is the smallest of the U.S. military service branches in terms of membership, the U.S. Coast Guard by itself is the world's 12th largest naval force.

1. The International Ship and Port Facility Security (ISPS) Code is an amendment to the Safety of Life at Sea (SOLAS) Convention (1974/1988) on minimum security arrangements for ships, ports and government agencies. Having come into force in 2004, it prescribes responsibilities to governments, shipping companies, shipboard personnel, and port/facility personnel to "detect security threats and take preventative measures against security incidents affecting ships or port facilities used in international trade.

The ISPS Code states that it is the sole responsibility of the Company Security Officer (CSO) and Company to approve the Ship Security Officer (SSO). This process must be approved by the administration of the flag state of the ship or verified security organization with approval of the Ship Security Plan or Vessel Security Plan (VSP).The ISPS Code ensures that before the VSP is set in place that Vessel Security Assessments must be taken (VSA).The Vessel Security Plan must address every requirement in the Vessel Security Assessment. The VSP must establish a number of important roles and steps to provide safety for the marine vessel. Therefore, the VSP must include procedures to allow necessary communication that shall be enforced at all times. The VSP has to include procedures that assessed for the performance of daily security protocols. It also must include the assessment of security surveillance equipment systems to detect malfunctioning parts. ISPS code requires that the Vessel Security Plan must have strict procedure and practices for the vital protection of Sensitive Security Information (SSI) that is either in the form of electronic or paper. Observation of procedures has to include timed submissions, and assessments of security reports pertaining to heightened security concerns. ISPS code requests that the VSP maintain an updated inventory of dangerous or hazardous goods and substances that are carried aboard the ship. The location of the goods or substance must be stated in the inventory report.

2. Surface and Maritime Transportation Security Act

This bill requires the Transportation Security Administration (TSA) to:

(1) Assess, and implement a risk-based security strategy to address, the vulnerabilities of and risks to surface transportation and maritime transportation systems;

(2) Develop a management oversight strategy that identifies the parties responsible for implementing the security strategy; and

(3) Submit a report that describes a risk-based budget and resource allocation plan for surface transportation sectors that reflects the security strategy.

The TSA shall establish the Surface Transportation Security Advisory Committee to make recommendations pertaining to surface transportation security.

In addition, the bill:

- Directs the Department of Homeland Security (DHS) to expand the TSA's explosives detection canine team program and to deploy next generation technologies to detect nuclear material,

- Requires the Government Accountability Office to study specified matters related to surface transportation,

- Expands the permissible uses of railroad security improvement grants,

- Requires the TSA to issue a decision on the use of a passenger vetting system by the National Railroad Passenger Corporation (Amtrak),

- Requires the TSA to establish a program to promote surface transportation security through the training of surface transportation operators and frontline employees,

- Expands the transportation security card program to allow individuals subject to credentialing or a background check to apply for a transportation security card, and

- Requires DHS to evaluate cargo-container scanning technologies.

The bill authorizes appropriations for FY2018-FY2021 for DHS to award surface transportation preparedness grants, subject to specified certification requirements.

CSI addresses the threat to border security and global trade posed by the potential for terrorist use of a maritime container to deliver a weapon. CSI proposes a security regime to ensure all containers that pose a potential risk for terrorism are identified and inspected at foreign ports before they are placed on vessels destined for the United States. CBP has stationed teams of U.S. CBP Officers in foreign locations to work together with our host foreign government counterparts. Their mission is to target and prescreen containers and to develop additional investigative leads related to the terrorist threat to cargo destined to the United States.

The three core elements of CSI are:

- Identify high-risk containers. CBP uses automated targeting tools to identify containers that pose a potential risk for terrorism, based on advance information and strategic intelligence.

- Prescreen and evaluate containers before they are shipped. Containers are screened as early in the supply chain as possible, generally at the port of departure.

- Use technology to prescreen high-risk containers to ensure that screening can be done rapidly without slowing down the movement of trade. This technology includes large-scale X-ray and gamma ray machines and radiation detection devices.

Through CSI, CBP officers work with host customs administrations to establish security criteria for identifying high-risk containers. Those administrations use non-intrusive inspection (NII) and radiation detection technology to screen high-risk containers before they are shipped to U.S. ports.

Announced in January 2002, CSI has made great strides since its inception. A significant number of customs administrations have committed to joining CSI and operate at various stages of implementation.

CSI is now operational at ports in North America, Europe, Asia, Africa, the Middle East, and Latin and Central America. CBP's 58 operational CSI ports now prescreen over 80 percent of all maritime containerized cargo imported into the United States.

Rules implementation

Phasing into new regulations is putting stress on many shipowners and shipping companies, because though there are around a hundred ballast water treatment systems available on the market, only six of these systems are approved by the IMO. This makes it difficult for shipowners to adopt systems that both satisfy IMO regulations and fit the specificities of their ships. The US Coast Guard in particular has placed special emphasis on ships having "USCG type-approved ballast water management systems or an approved Alternative Management System (AMS). After five years, the AMS must either achieve USCG type-approval or be replaced with a type-approved system" (Ship-Technology). These guidelines are being strictly enforced on both US flag ships as well as foreign ships that operate in US waters. Though the IMO is less strict, it is clear that the world recognizes the dangers of ballast water.

Invasive aquatic species present a major threat to the marine ecosystems, and shipping has been identified as a major pathway for introducing species to new environments. The problem increased as trade and traffic volume expanded over the last few decades, and in particular with the introduction of steel hulls, allowing vessels to use water instead of solid materials as ballast. The effects of the introduction of new species have in many areas of the world been devastating. Quantitative data show the rate of bio-invasions is continuing to increase at an alarming rate. As the volumes of seaborne trade continue overall to increase, the problem may not yet have reached its peak.

However, the Ballast Water Management Convention, adopted in 2004, aims to prevent the spread of harmful aquatic organisms from one region to another, by establishing standards and procedures for the management and control of ships' ballast water and sediments.

Under the Convention, all ships in international traffic are required to manage their ballast water and sediments to a certain standard, according to a ship-specific ballast water management plan. All ships will also have to carry a ballast water record book and an international ballast water management certificate. The ballast water management standards will be phased in over a period of time. As an intermediate solution, ships should exchange ballast water mid-ocean. However, eventually most ships will need to install an on-board ballast water treatment system.

A number of guidelines have been developed to facilitate the implementation of the Convention.

The Convention will require all ships to implement a Ballast Water and Sediments Management Plan. All ships will have to carry a Ballast Water Record Book and will be required to carry out ballast water management procedures to a given standard. Existing ships will be required to do the same, but after a phase-in period.

Parties to the Convention are given the option to take additional measures which are subject to criteria set out in the Convention and to IMO guidelines

The Convention is divided into Articles; and an Annex which includes technical standards and requirements in the Regulations for the control and management of ships' ballast water and sediments.

General Obligations

Under Article 2 General Obligations Parties undertake to give full and complete effect to the provisions of the Convention and the Annex in order to prevent, minimize and ultimately eliminate the transfer of harmful aquatic organisms and pathogens through the control and management of ships' ballast water and sediments.

Parties are given the right to take, individually or jointly with other Parties, more stringent measures with respect to the prevention, reduction or elimination of the transfer of harmful aquatic organisms and pathogens through the control and management of ships' ballast water and sediments, consistent with international law. Parties should ensure that ballast water management practices do not cause greater harm than they prevent to their environment, human health, property or resources, or those of other States.

Reception facilities

Under Article 5 Sediment Reception Facilities Parties undertake to ensure that ports and terminals where cleaning or repair of ballast tanks occurs, have adequate reception facilities for the reception of sediments.

Research and monitoring

Article 6 Scientific and Technical Research and Monitoring calls for Parties individually or jointly to promote and facilitate scientific and technical research on ballast water management; and monitor the effects of ballast water management in waters under their jurisdiction.

Survey, certification and inspection

Ships are required to be surveyed and certified (Article 7 Survey and certification) and may be inspected by port State control officers (Article 9 Inspection of Ships) who can verify that the ship has a valid certificate; inspect the Ballast Water Record Book; and/or sample the ballast water. If there are concerns, then a detailed inspection may be carried out and "the Party carrying out the inspection shall take such steps as will ensure that the ship shall not discharge Ballast Water until it can do so without presenting a threat of harm to the environment, human health, property or resources."

All possible efforts shall be made to avoid a ship being unduly detained or delayed.

Technical assistance

Under Article 13 Technical Assistance, Co-operation and Regional Co-operation, Parties undertake, directly or through the Organization and other international bodies, as appropriate, in respect of the control and management of ships' ballast water and sediments, to provide support for those Parties which request technical assistance to train personnel; to ensure the availability of relevant technology, equipment and facilities; to initiate joint research and development programmes; and to undertake other action aimed at the effective implementation of this Convention and of guidance developed by the Organization related thereto.

Annex - Section A General Provisions

This includes definitions, application and exemptions. Under Regulation A-2 General Applicability: "Except where expressly provided otherwise, the discharge of Ballast Water shall only be conducted through Ballast Water Management, in accordance with the provisions of this Annex."

Annex - Section B Management and Control Requirements for Ships

Ships are required to have on board and implement a Ballast Water Management Plan approved by the Administration (Regulation B-1). The Ballast Water Management Plan is specific to each ship and includes a detailed description of the actions to be taken to implement the Ballast Water Management requirements and supplemental Ballast Water Management practices.

Ships must have a Ballast Water Record Book (Regulation B-2) to record when ballast water is taken on board; circulated or treated for Ballast Water Management purposes; and discharged into the sea. It should also record when Ballast Water is discharged to a reception facility and accidental or other exceptional discharges of Ballast Water

The specific requirements for ballast water management are contained in regulation B-3 Ballast Water Management for Ships.

Other methods of ballast water management may also be accepted as alternatives to the ballast water exchange standard and ballast water performance standard, provided that such methods ensure at least the same level of protection to the environment, human health, property or resources, and are approved in principle by IMO's Marine Environment Protection Committee (MEPC).

Under Regulation B-4 Ballast Water Exchange, all ships using ballast water exchange should:

whenever possible, conduct ballast water exchange at least 200 nautical miles from the nearest land and in water at least 200 metres in depth, taking into account Guidelines developed by IMO;

in cases where the ship is unable to conduct ballast water exchange as above, this should be as far from the nearest land as possible, and in all cases at least 50 nautical miles from the nearest land and in water at least 200 metres in depth.

When these requirements cannot be met areas may be designated where ships can conduct ballast water exchange. All ships shall remove and dispose of sediments from spaces designated to carry ballast water in accordance with the provisions of the ships' ballast water management plan (Regulation B-4).

Annex - Section C Additional measures

A Party, individually or jointly with other Parties, may impose on ships additional measures to prevent, reduce, or eliminate the transfer of Harmful Aquatic Organisms and Pathogens through ships' Ballast Water and Sediments.

In these cases, the Party or Parties should consult with adjoining or nearby States that may be affected by such standards or requirements and should communicate their intention to establish additional measure(s) to the Organization at least 6 months, except in emergency or epidemic situations, prior to the projected date of implementation of the measure(s). When appropriate, Parties will have to obtain the approval of IMO.

Annex - Section D Standards for Ballast Water Management

There is a ballast water exchange standard and a ballast water performance standard. Ballast water exchange could be used to meet the performance standard:

Regulation D-1 Ballast Water Exchange Standard - Ships performing Ballast Water exchange shall do so with an efficiency of 95 per cent volumetric exchange of Ballast Water. For ships exchanging ballast water by the pumping-through method, pumping through three times the volume of each ballast water tank shall be considered to meet the standard described. Pumping through less than three times the volume may be accepted provided the ship can demonstrate that at least 95 percent volumetric exchange is met.

Regulation D-2 Ballast Water Performance Standard - Ships conducting ballast water management shall discharge less than 10 viable organisms per cubic metre greater than or equal to 50 micrometres in minimum dimension and less than 10 viable organisms per milliliter less than 50 micrometres in minimum dimension and greater than or equal to 10 micrometres in minimum dimension; and discharge of the indicator microbes shall not exceed the specified concentrations.

The indicator microbes, as a human health standard, include, but are not be limited to:

a. Toxicogenic Vibrio cholerae (O1 and O139) with less than 1 colony forming unit (cfu) per 100 milliliters or less than 1 cfu per 1 gram (wet weight) zooplankton samples ;

b. Escherichia coli less than 250 cfu per 100 milliliters;

c. Intestinal Enterococci less than 100 cfu per 100 milliliters.

Ballast Water Management systems must be approved by the Administration in accordance with IMO Guidelines (Regulation D-3 Approval requirements for Ballast Water Management systems). These include systems which make use of chemicals or biocides; make use of organisms or biological mechanisms; or which alter the chemical or physical characteristics of the Ballast Water.

Prototype technologies

Regulation D-4 covers Prototype Ballast Water Treatment Technologies. It allows for ships participating in a programme approved by the Administration to test and evaluate promising Ballast Water treatment technologies to have a leeway of five years before having to comply with the requirements.

Review of standards

Under regulation D-5 Review of Standards by the Organization, IMO is required to review the Ballast Water Performance Standard, taking into account a number of criteria including safety considerations; environmental acceptability, i.e., not causing more or greater environmental impacts than it solves; practicability, i.e., compatibility with ship design and operations; cost effectiveness; and biological effectiveness in terms of removing, or otherwise rendering inactive harmful aquatic organisms and pathogens in ballast water. The review should include a determination of whether appropriate technologies are available to achieve the standard, an assessment of the above mentioned criteria, and an assessment of the socio-economic effect(s) specifically in relation to the developmental needs of developing countries, particularly small island developing States.

Annex- Section E Survey and Certification Requirements for Ballast Water Management

Gives requirements for initial renewal, annual, intermediate and renewal surveys and certification requirements. Appendices give form of Ballast Water Management Certificate and Form of Ballast Water Record Book.

ABOUT AUTHOR

Sunil Sarangi is an experienced Marine Engineer, He has founded Eco Marine, a Ballast Water Treatment Systems Design and consultants' firm that helps to protect and control aquatic invasive species.

He began working in the Ballast water regulation in the United States in the early 2005's. He received his bachelor's degree in Marine Engineering from the Birla Institute of Technology at India in 2004. He also, received his Master's of Science in Ocean Engineering from Florida Institute of Technology at Florida in 2008. As his carrier continued having a top stop, he bagged Master of Science in Ocean Engineering with a Bachelor of Science in Marine Engineering, and also MBA.

During the past decade his work has focused upon developing cost-effective methods for reducing the spread of aquatic invasive species, the economic cost of this introduction has been estimated by the U.S. Fish and Wildlife Service at about $5 billion.

His work over the past 10 years can be summarized as covering the following subjects:

- The design and development of Ballast Water Treatment Systems

- Investigations into the effectiveness of techniques and technologies for measuring and reducing aquatic nuisance species.

- As a lead manager, successfully completed more than $40 million USD projects related to Ballast Water Treatment Systems.

Mr. Sunil Sarangi has authored several articles on Marine engineering and Ballast Water Treatment issues and has spoken at numerous symposia and conferences during the past decade.